Write
for *your* life

Discovering and revealing
who you are today

By Shirley Anstis

Words and photographs © Shirley Anstis 2009
Published by lulu.com 2009

All rights reserved. No part of this publication may be reproduced, stored in a retrieval system, or transmitted, in any form without the prior permission in writing of the author.

*This book is dedicated to my sister
Jennifer Jones, who lived a full life
in her 36 years.*

For a life worth living, my beautiful son,

Yours
Mum xxx
16/8/11

Acknowledgements

Thank you to Megan Weston for working with me to make this book look so beautiful. Thank you to Rachel Greenbank and Sam Warren for offering suggestions. Thank you to my soul sisters Zenobi Bynoe and Juliet Carr for their encouraging feedback. Thank you also to Diana Mackarill and my sister Julia Jones, whose comments on the first draft made me want to do it better. Thank you to the lovely John Brown who agreed to do a foreword for this book. And finally, thanks to my husband Laurie who is always encouraging and supportive.

Foreword

Life is made up of questions and answers, and how we respond and react to questions of life will determine our character and personality. In her book Shirley Anstis speaks from her own personal experiences to challenge us to be open and honest to the questions we are facing as part of our every day life.

This is a book for all of us to read no matter our age (I'm in my 60's); it is easy to read and to dip into whenever we are faced up to different issues of life such as: personality, relationships and responsibilities, bereavement, family life, and finances.

I have fully enjoyed reading Shirley's manuscript and believe this book will be very useful for people of all ages and backgrounds to have on their shelves.

John Brown
MANAGER OF GREYFRIARS BOOKSHOP
AND PRISON CHAPLAIN

Contents

Where I am today 13
Why read this book 16
What this book offers 18
How to use this book 21

Art 26
Attitude 30
Behaviour 33
Body 36
Care 42
Death 45
Effort and Energy 49
Faith or Fate 53
God 57
Health 62

Home 65

Honesty 69

Hope 71

Identity 74

Journey 78

Kindness 82

Laughter 86

Love 89

Money 93

Mothers and Fathers 96

Nature 99

Openness 103

Passion 108

Personality 112

Play 117

Quiet spaces 120

Relationships 124

Responsibility 129

Safety 133

Soul 137

Thinking 139

Time 142

Understanding 145

Values 148

Will 152

Witness 155

e(X)press 157

Yearning 161

Zero tolerance 164

Ending 168

Our Greatest Fear 172

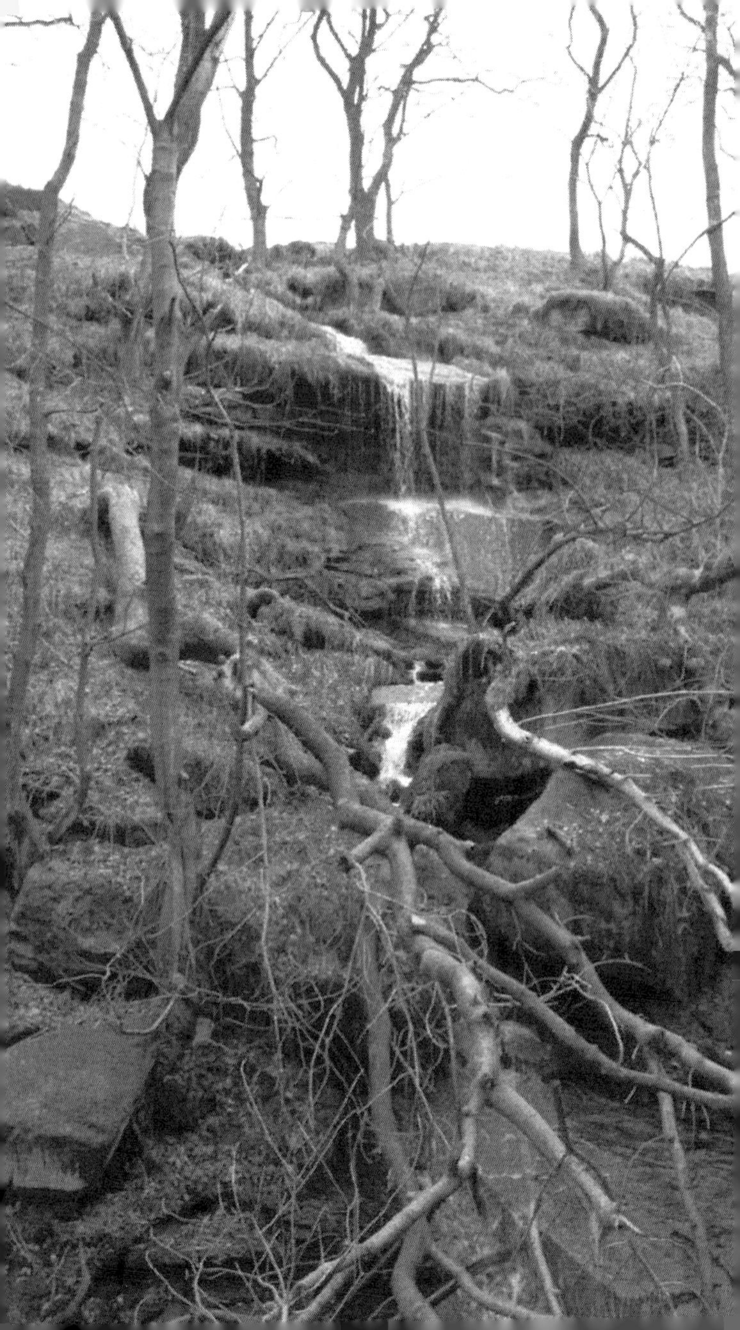

Where I am today

I have come to a point in my life where I am trying to be truly who I am, how I was created. I am trying to live authentically and be true to myself. That is not as selfish or as self-conscious as it sounds because it frees me up to be real with people and respond to them honestly. Most of us respond to others as though everyone is like us but if we spend time understanding ourselves we will realise that we are truly unique.

Once I started to explore my inner world I found I became less scared of the world and more confident of my own ability to cope with the world. It also allows me to be connected to my values and be honest with myself. Although it seems counter- intuitive, such time spent understanding myself helps me to have time and patience in trying to understand others. What is good for me is good for them too. When I feel comfortable in my own skin then life is exciting, spontaneous, meaningful and rich. It is not about being self-conscious but being aware of the impact I have on others and they have on me. It is about me trying to be my best self and live in community as a fellow human being with all my gifts and flaws.

I feel I am on a continuous learning cycle in my journey of life. One lesson gives way to another and there is always something new to understand, embrace and reflect on. I have changed countries and changed careers yet whilst some parts of me have changed and grown other parts remain as they were in my youth.

We absorb things from our parents and early environment and we don't realise what we have picked up until we come up against people who have had a completely different start in life. They think, feel and behave differently from us.

I used to be very shy. Through faith, friendship and therapy I have become more relaxed in my life. I can still be shy but it feels different.

Why read this book?

I am sharing this with you in the hope that you value your time here on earth and have a desire to be on your own unique path. There are some questions that we all need to look at to help us live our best life. These questions could be addressed consciously.

By reading this you will begin to make your personal outlook more visible to yourself and as a result you will feel more secure in who and how you are. This allows you to become sure of what you think and feel, or to admit that you do not know and begin to explore possible answers. The answers are only important to you and no one will be checking up on you. The alternative is to go through life never knowing who you are, what you do and why you do it. You could live a long life and then wonder what you did with your time. You could find yourself unhappy in later life and wonder where it all went wrong. Or you could start now and make the best use of the time you have left.

Modern life has become much more complex than it was. Lifestyle is no longer a fixed idea but something we need to make choices about. The world offers so many different ways of existing that we need to decide what kind of life we would like to have. Work, family and relationships are all being redefined and you need to know what it means to you. Is it about making money or being an activist? Are friends more like family to you and can you have more than one home? These are just a few of the questions this book will raise in your mind.

What this book offers

This book can help you to stand back from your life and take an objective look at it. It does not tell you what sort of life you should have. It just encourages you to become aware of the life that you are living. If you are aware then you can make changes or you can try to stop changes. Either way, awareness helps.

Most of us leave home without ever thinking about the life we want in the world. Often we use our parents as examples of what we do or do not want to achieve. But to base our whole life on copying or rejecting seems so random. Surely it's worth having a broader approach and more examples to choose from. Through biographies, blogs and other media we have access to the lives of many people. They can be seen as encouraging examples or role models for different aspects of our lives.

This is not about copying anyone but seeing a range of what is possible. I am not talking of money and fame but personal attributes like dedication and the modern phenomenon: work-life balance.

At this stage in your life you may be going through a transition from one way of being to another. It could be that this is triggered by: moving home, a new significant relationship, changing the makeup of your household, a new job or training endeavour or changes in what you are physically able to do. It may feel like you have been here before or it might feel completely new. Whatever the case, this book will help you to look at things anew.

Congratulations for being brave enough to pick up this book. You obviously value your life and you wish to live it with awareness. You are open to exploring who you are now and who you might become in the future. This book is only a gentle start and there are many other ways of exploring who you are. It is never about fitting in to someone's idea of who you should be but about going deeper within yourself to discover the beautiful and unique person you were created to be.

'You are the light of the world. A city on a hill cannot be hidden. Neither do people light a lamp and put it under a bowl. Instead they put it on its stand, and it gives light to everyone in the house. In the same way, let your light shine before men, that they may see your good deeds and praise your Father in heaven.'
MATTHEW CHAPTER 5 VERSES 14−16 IN THE BIBLE (NEW INTERNATIONAL VERSION)

How to use this book

This book came to me as a clear idea in one of my most creative moments. I have organised it alphabetically because that was the way in which I managed my thinking process at the time. Anything else feels overly structured and artificial.

Each letter of the alphabet covers some aspect of life that I feel is important. If you got to the end of your years and no one mentioned love to you then you will be very disappointed. You may decide it is too much work to explore your life, or that you will get around to it when you are older, but wouldn't it be great to spend the time now so that you can have an impact on your future direction in the world? Part of me wishes someone had given me this book when I was in my twenties.

Although I have written the book as a coherent whole I suggest you read small chunks at a time. Don't feel the need to read it in one sitting as that can feel quite overwhelming. You may just want to see what areas it covers and then work on these areas gradually. You do not have to work on all areas at once. You can discuss this with people you care about and see if they've reflected on these things. You can read around the areas highlighted and come to your own conclusions. However you approach this topic, your life will demonstrate what you think, feel and do. Whatever decisions you make now will affect you and those close to you, now and in the future.

You can see each letter as a section and read a section at a time. Some letters have more items than others because there were things

I thought I had to include if this book is going to be of any use. At the opposite end I found it challenging to think of an essential life perspective which begins with X or Z! There were more things I could include overall but then it would be a much bigger and more complex book. I'd happily write that one next.

For each topic, reflect on what it means to you, why it means that and how your life supports what you believe. Is there a balance in your approach towards this thing or is it skewed in one direction? Who in your life – close or distant – can be an example in this area? How would you like this part of your life to develop over time?

I have provided some questions to begin your reflections and given you some space to jot down initial responses. Any or all of these could be followed up with reading, discussion and therapy. It is up to you what you decide to do next.

Take time out. Read slowly. Leave space between the topics to allow them to breathe in you. Take what will help. Leave what will not. You choose which aspects of your life you wish to explore and for how long. I often think that life is about learning something new, being affected by it and responding to it. This book could be helpful wherever you are in your journey. What happens next is up to YOU.

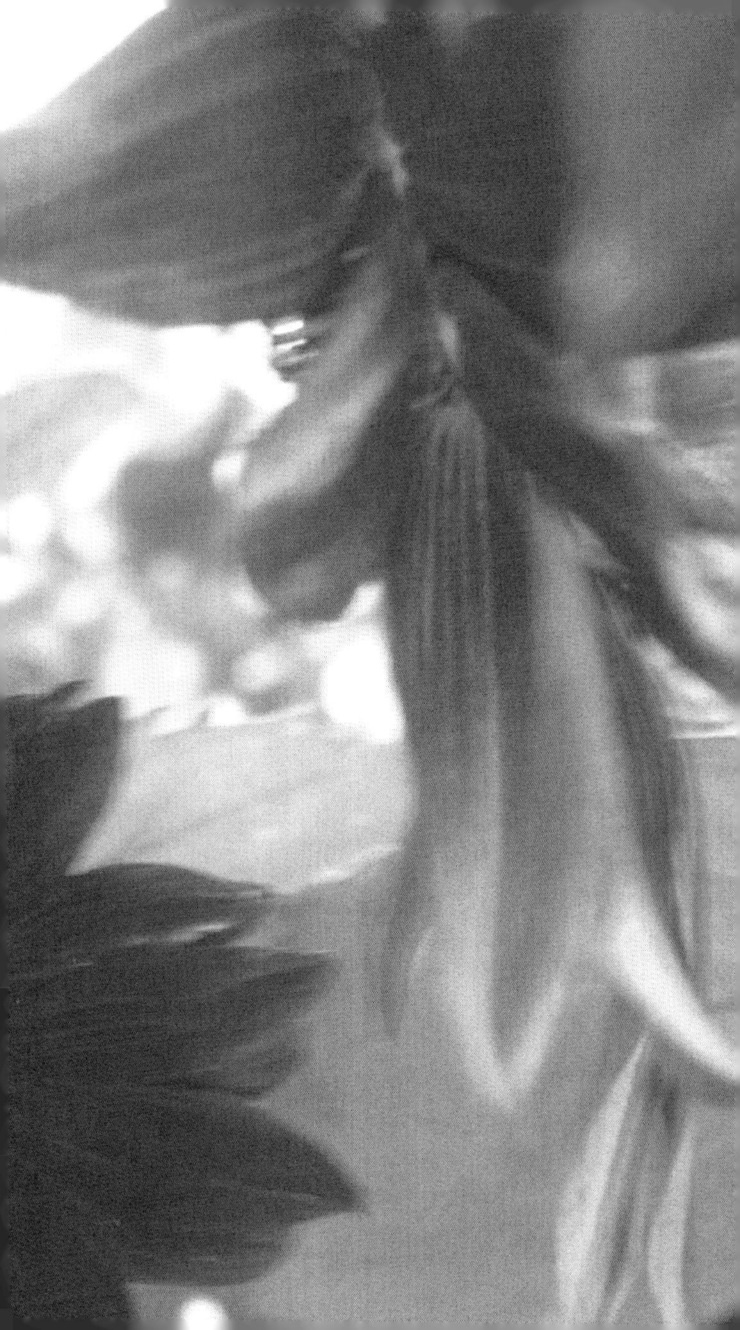

Art

Have you ever wondered about what you know and what you do not know in life? Sometimes I stumble upon insights and it surprises me that I did not know that thing before. Art is all around us even though we do not always see it.

Classically it is about paintings and drawings that have been done by great artists. It can also be about sculpture and other images. For some it is about a literal interpretation of a real thing or event whilst for others it can be about creating a mood or a feeling. Some people get very excited about what counts as art and what does not.

For me it is an opportunity to appreciate the image and the emotions it connects to. I love a good painting or sculpture although I can't really do either myself. I do however enjoy taking photographs and have been very pleased to include my photos in this book. Images can stir us on a very deep level and help us to appreciate the complexity of our existence. I love to pop in to art galleries and museums in my lunch hour as it sometimes puts the day's work into perspective and reminds me that there is more to life than whatever I am working on.

What we call art seems to be changing and expanding all the time. I went to see a very modern exhibition recently and found it very engaging. I decided to enter into the fun of it and not stand aside critising it. There were mounds of concrete and weird mirrors that contorted reality. Other recent events have seen someone running in a gallery and people performing on a plinth as forms of living art.

As modern western life becomes more designed I think art is moving off the walls and into our homes and lives. Art influences the designs of chairs, kitchens, cars and trainers. It could be the way a dish is served in a restaurant or the beautiful movement of a world-class dancer. We all consume art in our daily lives. Art meets fashion on the high street. I often see gorgeous shoes that are beautiful to look at but impossible to wear. Art meets nature in sunrise and sunset.

Thankfully we do not need to create or own art to appreciate it. How does the idea of art sound to you? Is this something you have an appreciation for or does it seem unnecessary and foolish? What do you consider art? Are you able to appreciate any art in your life?

✎ …

Attitude

So what is your attitude towards art and to your life as a whole? It is the simple things that can sometimes make a big difference in how we approach life.

I really think if we shared our insights and learning more it could have a wonderfully contagious and healing effect. It is a much better gift to share than negativity, irritation, superficiality, self-importance and other non-uplifting attitudes. Our attitude is a key aspect of what we put into life. That attitude also affects what we get out of it. It impacts on our relationships with others, how they experience us and how we perceive them. Are we open and positive or closed off and negative? If you believe that like attracts like then positivity from us brings that out in others. Similarly, negativity attaches to negativity. Individually we are part of this multiplying effect that spreads through society. Some people pay attention to an approach called the law of attraction which suggests that you can attract into your life that which you seek by being focused on it. It suggests that we have an impact on our world – it matters how we are.

'If you don't like something, change it. If you can't change it, change your attitude'. Maya Angelou. Are you aware of the attitudes you carry around with you? How would the people in your life describe your attitudes? Is this what you feel is true for you or does it feel like circumstances cause you to respond in certain ways? Has your attitude made life difficult for you? How would it be to talk to the people in your life who you trust and get them to give you some feedback on this? Is there anything else you'd like to consider as a result of reading this?

✏️ ...

Behaviour

It is not just about attitude. Our behaviour matters too. There is no point saying all the right things, and then not following through with our actions. Our behaviour is what the world sees of our heart. The world sees our works and imagines what our heart is like.

Not only does our behaviour indicate who we are to others but also to ourselves. Sometimes we like to delude ourselves and think that we are different from how we really are but our behaviour provides evidence of the choices we make. There is an old saying that action speaks louder than words. This is difficult to dispute. In Christianity the Bible says that by their fruits you shall know them. Our fruits are what we give out to the world. That doesn't mean rushing around and being showy – doing to be noticed and praised. It is about connecting our behaviour to our attitude and being true about how we are working our way through the challenges that life presents.

How can we show who we are by what we do? Do you find you behave in ways that surprise you? Maybe you are doing things you do not really want to do or not doing things that you long to do? Would you like to explore what this means for you? It could be linked to something that happened in the past or something that is happening in your life now. Who can you talk to about this?

✎ ...

Body

Our bodies are so important to the pleasure we get out of life yet we often take them for granted. It is so important that we look after our body and have a good relationship with it.

Many of us try to ignore the reality of being in a human body with all its associated miracles and frailties.

So many people take better care of their possessions than their bodies yet bodies are not replaceable. This is not about beauty or expensive treatments but about the simple everyday task of looking after the container that carries us through the world. It is about a healthy diet, exercise, relaxation and sleep. Although there have been lots of fads in this area the core messages remain the same. We know we need vegetables and fruits (in a range of colours); regular exercise and a good night's sleep everyday. We also need to drink plenty of water to keep us hydrated. It was some years ago when I realized that I was not drinking enough water and the effect that would have on my body. I am still not very good at this but it has improved. I sometimes force myself to drink it. Thankfully I like other healthy drinks such as herbal teas and I do not drink fizzy drinks. It is not about being perfect but minimising the bad stuff we do to our bodies and maximising the good stuff. Like most things balance is also important and health is more about sensible moderation than extremes. Of course there may be times when we struggle to make healthy choices. That does not mean we should give up or feel guilty, but just use our awareness to help us to do our best. It's never useful to think in terms of all or nothing, every bit counts.

We know that smoking is bad for us and alcohol is best consumed in moderation. There are many other substances that can cause varying degrees of harm to our bodies and it is up to us what role these have in our lives. A lot is said about the addictive qualities of harmful substances but I think some healthy foods can be addictive too. I love nuts, seeds, fruits and fish – but not all together! None of these are unhealthy. The responsibility is back to you and the habits that you form.

Our bodies are very sophisticated. They can tolerate much neglect in our teens and twenties but if this continues then our bodies find ways of telling us that they are not happy (e.g. headaches, backaches). From eyes to teeth we need to have regular check-ups to know what is going on in our bodies and what we should be doing to acquire or maintain good health. As well as physical health our bodies also link in to our mental health and sense of wellbeing. If we are in physical discomfort then it is challenging for us to feel upbeat about life. We can take in foods that affect our bodies in different ways: lifting our mood (chocolate), getting rid of bad stuff (antioxidants) and introducing good stuff (omega oils from oily fish and various seeds) for example.

You may need to learn to love the body you have been given and not compare it to others. Sometimes it can be good to think of what your body can do (e.g. hike, run, swim, give birth) rather than how it looks. You may have more serious body issues that are linked with mental health concerns and I would suggest you seek help for this. Eating disorders can be overcome. Whatever the case our bodies are key to our physical and, to some extent, mental health and we need to be taking notice of how they are functioning and what impact our attention or neglect is having.

How do you feel about your body and how you treat it? Would you say that you value the body you have been given or are you more likely to be found neglecting or criticising it? Do you expose your body to harm? When did you last visit the dentist or do some physical activity? What might be your first step to looking after your body?

✏️ ...

Care

I imagine life is more interesting if we care about something and/or someone. It starts with self-care otherwise we may not be around long enough to care for anyone or anything else. But self-care alone can lead to a very narrow existence.

Care is more than meeting physical needs. It could also be about our emotional, spiritual and financial needs. Once we begin to care about one aspect of our life then we begin to realise the other areas we have been neglecting. Again it is all about steps in the right direction not about trying to be perfect.

We are so enamoured by celebrity these days that we expect people to spend all day dieting, exercising, exfoliating, massaging, shopping and dressing to radiate perfection. How incredibly self-centred we expect them to be! Or we expect them to roll out of bed looking perfect even though we have never found that for ourselves. Maybe we are so interested in how they look because it distracts us from ourselves.

When we take care of ourselves we will encourage others to do the same. This could have a good impact on our friends and relations as we encourage them to look after themselves. We might then begin to care about some aspect of our world. With globalisation we are all more interconnected than ever, whether that is food resources, financial markets, technology or the environment. As such, caring for others is also in our best interest.

So, do you care about yourself? Is there any one or any thing that you also care about? Are you able to demonstrate this through what you do and say? Do you care about nothing and don't see the point? Is there someone you can speak to or a book you can read? There are great psychotherapists, philosophers, theologians and other social scientists who can share their perspectives with you. This could be a start to finding your own passions.

✎ ...

Death

Sadly for all of us dying is an aspect of living. It is inevitable, regardless of our attitudes, behaviour or caring. None of us are infinite. Death comes, whether slow or fast, gentle or chaotic, expected or shocking. So how do we live with this certainty?

For me, this is something that has changed over time. Although I have always known that young people could die, the experience of my family and friends has always been that one got old and then one died. Then my youngest sister passed away very suddenly. What is that about? What does it mean? Am I on borrowed time? What am I here for? What shall I do with this 'extra' time? This was my specific process in facing my newfound conscious awareness of my future death.

Of course, we will not mourn our own death, others will. What would you like to offer to the world, to leave behind before that fateful day? Now is the time to start thinking about this. For me it does not mean being depressed or particularly serious but recognising that we cannot take our life for granted so we need to prioritise what we would like to do and try our best to live the way we feel called to – our soul's unique journey. Maybe we have a special gift for the world and whilst we waste time trying to copy everyone else our gift is not being used or seen but remains hidden.

Here is a quote that encourages us to explore our individual gifts and the impact that has on us collectively:

Just as each of us has one body with many members, and these members do not all have the same function, so in Christ we who are many form one body and each member belongs to all others. We have different gifts, according to the grace given us. If a man's gift is in prophesying, let him use it in proportion to his faith. If it is serving, let him serve; if it is teaching, let him teach; if it is encouraging, let him encourage; if it is contributing to the needs of others, let him give generously; if it is leadership, let him govern diligently; if it is showing mercy, let him do it cheerfully.'
ROMANS CHAPTER 12, VERSES 3(B)−8, IN THE BIBLE
(NEW INTERNATIONAL VERSION)

It would be wonderful if we could all offer our gifts to the world before it is too late. Together we can have a big impact on our world.

If you consider that you will not be alive forever how do you feel? This is not something you need to think about but it might help if you feel lost and purposeless. What would you like to do with your time here on earth? Are you concerned about what happens after death and does that impact on how you view your life?

✏️ ...

Effort and Energy

Well no doubt you are beginning to feel that life really takes effort and energy. It does but it can be a cyclical process where the energy supports the effort and such effort encourages more energetic responses.

It is about the energy we give off when we meet others and that which we pick up from them. We have our own natural energy levels but that gets drained when we are surrounded by people, places or things that do not encourage us to reveal who we are. A lifetime of that could really take its toll and leave a person feeling completely depleted. In such circumstances a recharge is necessary before any energy could be found, let alone emitted. So if all this sounds too heavy and laborious, maybe you need a retreat, a chance to rediscover yourself and what you want to put into and get out of life.

Think of your favourite person – how would you describe the energy they give off when you are with them? What about your least favourite person – what is their energy like? And what about you – how would others experience your energy or lack of?

Effort can have a bad name but there is nothing wrong in trying to achieve something. Most of us admire people who build something from nothing through their own effort. I am not suggesting forcing ourselves to be constantly heroic by ignoring our human frailty but success after effort can be very good for self-esteem and brings about a sense of empowerment. I remember how great I felt after passing my driving test having had several attempts. Although I found it more difficult than academic study I knew it was important for a more confident adult life. It gives me more options about what, when and how I participate in the world. Both energy and effort helps to move our life forward rather than allowing us to stay in some early form of development for our whole life. Life has a lot to offer but generally things tend not to fall into our laps. Although it may seem so for others that is not the case. Apart from winning a lottery most people work hard to get somewhere or to stay somewhere.

Are there any issues in your life you have ignored or avoided because you did not want to put in the effort? Was this from a real need to protect yourself or some less admirable reason? Is there anything you would like in your life now if only you could put the effort in?

✎ …

Faith or Fate

What are we moving forward towards? Some of us have faith and this belief helps to hold us in times of uncertainty. Others believe in fate and that enables them to take an appropriate stance when making plans for their future.

For each of us it is something to lean on and it enables us to have hopes, plans, goals and aspirations. Neither approach guarantees predictability so we can only do our best and leave the rest up to God, fate or spirit – depending on our perspective on things. 'Faith is taking the first step even when you don't see the whole staircase.' Martin Luther King Jr.

Another viewpoint is that offered by meditative religions such as Buddhism, where mindfulness and being in the moment is key to one's approach to life. If your particular personality gets so caught up in worries about the future that you cannot focus on anything in the immediate present then it would benefit you to develop the ability to be in the moment. If, on the other hand, you have a healthy respect for the present and can give it the attention it deserves then you might want to develop the ability to have an eye on your future and appreciate how your current choices might impact on your future. Not in such a way that it paralyses you from doing anything, but just that you weigh up things and make the best choice you are capable of. When I worked as a school's careers adviser I remember some of the more academic students being particularly stressed about their future. They expected so much of themselves that they seemed to want guarantees that, for example, a language degree would get them to the UN or a business degree would get them a career in the City of London. Neither faith nor fate can tell us what will happen to us in our lifetime. In The Soul's Code James Hillman speaks of life being 'foreodained yet not foretold.'

So do you have faith in anyone or anything? How do you keep hope when the evidence is not always visible? Are you so scared of being disappointed that you believe in nothing and no one? How does that affect your day-to-day choices? Is this an area you would like to explore in more detail? You can start by sharing your thoughts with someone else and see where that leads.

✏️ ...

God

And so faithfulness brings us to an idea of God. It is possible to have some religious beliefs, to have none or to be unsure about what you believe.

Whatever the case it seems a sign of maturity is to give yourself some time to reflect on the questions and come to a sense of truth for yourself. At some point it is helpful for us to have a sense of why we are here, how we can use our life and what might happen in an afterlife. For some faiths it is about spreading God's word, whether that is a Jewish, Christian or Islamic god. Other faiths are about peaceful coexistence and views of an afterlife that may include reincarnation. For some without religious belief it is all about now: we are born, we live and we die. Some beliefs pay special attention to the individual (Buddhism), the family (Christianity) and the community (Islam). This is a very simplistic glance at who or what God might be to you. There are libraries dedicated to the great faiths of the world and I suggest you begin to explore what your beliefs are. We may develop our faith from the family we are born into, our cultural heritage, as part of the greater culture to which we belong or as a part of a personal journey. Such soul or spiritual seeking can lead to various experiences of acceptance and rejection by you and to you. Eventually you may find an approach that feels true to you.

Belief and faith can be very nuanced and individual things as they are not externally provable to those who do not believe. It is possible to belong to a faith and not believe every aspect of it; some people are more literal than others. 'Faith is not belief. Belief is passive. Faith is active.' Edith Hamilton.

Myths and stories also play a vital role in elaborating on the human experience. In my experience faith is not just about good and bad and sin and forgiveness, it could also be about the value of life and stewardship of the earth's resources or human rights and equality of opportunity for all human beings. Whatever faith or God we believe in we are human and we are imperfect. We may have godlike qualities but that is not all of who we are. I find it sad when people decide against a belief because they have met fallible representatives of that faith. If we can accept that there are imperfect parents, children, learners, teachers and doctors why can't we accept imperfect Christians and Muslims? Human imperfections encourage us to trust in our God and not rely on our own limited resources. Our approach of all or nothing does not give us choices but limits our experiences.

Of course there are those who would say that they have nothing to do with God or belief. Yet I believe there is that spiritual hole within all of us and we find something to fill it with. This becomes our god by another name. As I write this I can think of many such gods including money, politics, sport, art, nature, work, fame, power etc. People of faith could also participate in these aspects of life but their motivation and relation to it could be different. It is not always what we do but why and how we do it.

So who or what is your god? What do you believe in and put all your effort into understanding and following? I am not here to judge you for it but to encourage you to be aware of what it is for yourself. There is no need to tell the world but it helps you to know what you choose to believe and how that affects your subsequent decisions. All belief is about faith: nothing will be proved 100% otherwise it would simply be a fact and not a question of faith. Some of us believe. Eventually we will know. Others feel and think that there is nothing to believe. Find out what you believe and share it with those you care about and who care about you.

✎ …

Health

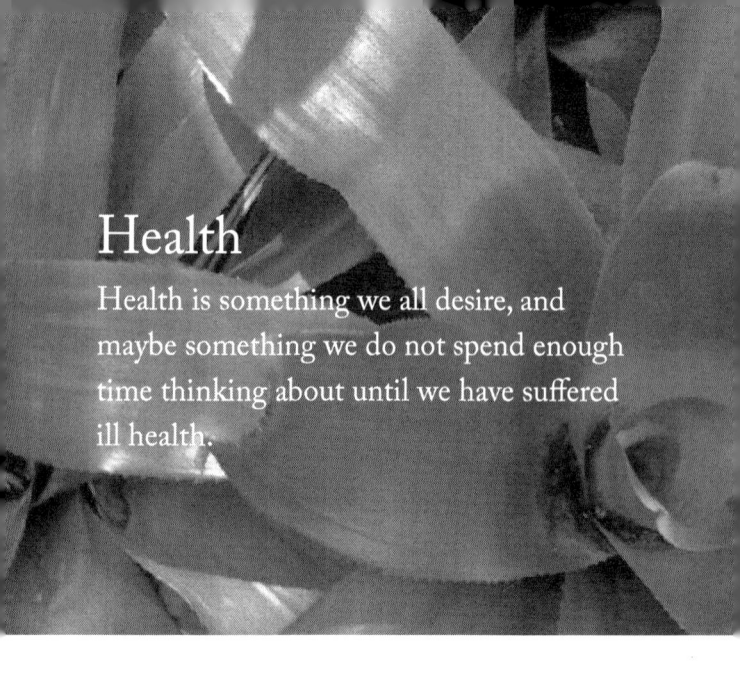

Health is something we all desire, and maybe something we do not spend enough time thinking about until we have suffered ill health.

I feel everyone should be informed and encouraged to look after their health from a young age. There is a lot being done across the world but many people continue to ignore their health and pretend they do not know what to do. I despair at the exporting of unhealthy foods from the developed world to the developing. I am sad when I visit the Caribbean and see people replacing healthy local food for mass-produced low-grade imports. This is particularly true of sweets where the homemade coconut fudge or nutmeg jam is thrown aside for a coloured chemical combination that contains no identifiable foods.

Like our health, we do not always value what we have until it disappears. Because of the global economic climate many of us have rediscovered the joys of locally produced and home-cooked meals. This is not only cheaper but often healthier as well. Some of us are also slowing down and fast food is being replaced by slow cooked meals.

Health is not only about the state of our bodies but also about our mental health, which covers our mind and emotions. Our emotions show us how we are responding to things in our life. We can make space for the range of our emotions, from joy to despair. Begin to be aware of what you pay attention to and what you ignore. Some of us can be quite obsessive about one aspect of our health, such as our diet, whilst another area is completely ignored. Take time to review how you take care of the health of your whole self. It does not matter where you start but the message is to get started. This is not about self-absorption but supports you to live a full and vibrant life. It also means that you are more likely to be around for the loved ones in your life.

✎…

Home

This brings me to the idea of home: a place where you care about others and they care about you. For me that is a more important concept than to say it is the place where you live. For many it is a simple concept; you grow up in your parents' home and then you go out and create your own.

A home needs to be more than a house because that is only a limited external combination of location, possessions and function. It could be about the community or country you feel a sense of belonging to. Home could be a community of likeminded people where tolerance and cultural exchange are encouraged. A home needs to offer some heart connection so that those who live there can be fully alive and feel supported. For me it is more of a sanctuary than a straightforward shelter. It is a place where I can unwind and I can offer hospitality to others.

England is becoming more like America in being more accepting of different migrant communities who maintain the culture of their home country whilst creating a new home in England; having two homes. I think of friends who have left England for South Africa, Australia and New Zealand in search of what they believe will be a new and better home for them. I think of Caribbean friends moving to America, England and Canada for the same reasons. I myself was born in England and grew up in the Caribbean. Where is home for me? Do I need to choose? In my experience, time spent, key relationships, commitments and a sense of belonging all have a part to play. Both England and the Caribbean have changed in the time I have been finding and creating my adult home.

There are many people without a sense of home even if they have lived in a land for several generations. They need to find a place that they can call home. Part of this I am sure is an ability to be at home with oneself. We would never find home if it is all about an expectation of the world continually welcoming us to some special place. We need to figure what we need and create that space in the world.

I know for me home is linked to a broader sense of identity and relationships. This may change over time as I continue to grow deeper into who I am and how I live my life. Listening to our specific desire for a place of refuge is part of our life's journey and one we should take seriously – no one can create a home for us. Similarly we do not need to recreate the home we grew up in although we could consciously choose to include aspects of that which we found supportive and, by the same token, leave out that which we did not. Have you found or created a home for yourself? Would you like to or does it seem unimportant?

✏️...

Honesty

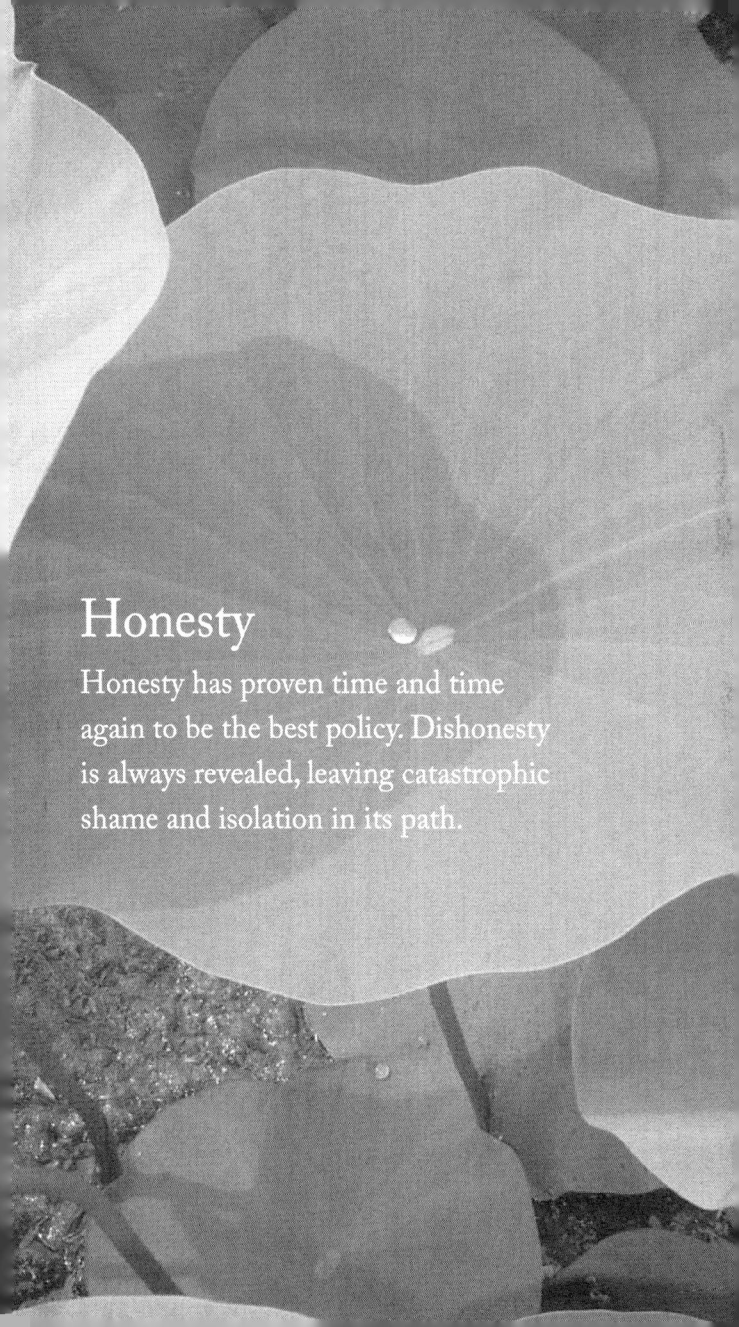

Honesty has proven time and time again to be the best policy. Dishonesty is always revealed, leaving catastrophic shame and isolation in its path.

Dishonesty would have a much more challenging impact on those we come into contact with as they would not be able to trust us. As well as this public side there is the internal turmoil of having to pretend to be someone that we are not – this takes a toll on our sense of who we are and on our happiness. Nothing is worth that damage to who we are.

Are you forever telling little lies to spare the feelings of others? Would you like the people in your life to be honest with you or do you only want to hear the good news?

✐ …

Hope

Hope helps me to believe in possibilities. It tells me that good things can and do happen and it is up to me to pay attention. Certainly this is a better way to approach life than feeling hopeless.

If we have hope we are more likely to put in effort and make plans for ourselves because we expect to make things happen. Of course hope does not mean things will happen the way we want them to but it puts us in a good frame of mind and encourages us to try; this is the first step to something occurring. 'We don't see things as they are, we see them as we are.' Anais Nin . Without hope we would not try.

Like everything else it is about balance. If something has proved unlikely to happen with our effort then there will be a time to accept this and move on. Hope is a starting point but it would be foolish to hold on to it when reality points the other way. We can redirect that effort elsewhere without feeling wronged or punished. Life has something better planned for us and we need to reach out and accept it.

Are you someone who is scared of hoping for anything because you fear being disappointed? Do you hope more for things you want to create or things you would like to be given?

✏️ ...

Identity

So who are you?
Do you feel you
know who you are?

In my work as a counsellor I find that underlying many problems is the sense that people do not know who they are. I myself have been exploring who I am in a more meaningful way. Each of us is unique; from the experiences of our early life, our family of origin, location of our early years and the backdrop of world events. These all have an impact on who we are and how we see ourselves. Some of this may seem quite random, but imagine being a teenager in Iraq during the last decade. Whatever the family stands for they cannot remove the impact of the community and the world. All of our past goes into who we are now. This may now determine where and how we choose to live our lives, what we do with our time and how we maintain our relationships. As we get older and the world continues to change we could find ourselves, and our sense of identity, in constant flux.

Our identity is about our sense of self and belonging, how we see ourselves and our place in the world. For me it is a complex thing that is not fully captured by those who see us from the outside. I truly believe that only we can explore our own unique identity.

For me it is about exploring and being connected to all the different aspects of who I am. So I am a woman and need to figure how

I relate to other women, both in our similarities and our differences. Similarly, how do I relate to men generally and specifically? As a Black Caribbean woman who lives a very British life how do I relate to Black British women of a different background, Caribbean women living elsewhere and British women who are not Black? – I have some similar experiences to all of these. It's about being aware of those points of connection. Add in faith, education, class, age and sexuality; these are all aspects of how I see myself and how the world might see me. But my internal sense of these observable identifiers may be different from that of the onlooker.

So how about you? What does it mean to be your specific gender, ethnicity, class, culture, sexuality and age? Do you have a difference that is hidden (e.g. deafness, epilepsy)? If you feel you are ordinary then imagine someone different from you in those identifiers. Do they remind you of someone in your social circle or someone you have never met and have strong opinions about? Only by truthfully looking at ourselves can we begin to figure out our identity. As we look deeper within we will have a better sense of the truth about who we are and how we relate to the rest of the world. For me it is about trying to connect to all parts of me, good and bad, and having people in my life who reflect different parts of that to me as I do for them.

✎ …

Journey

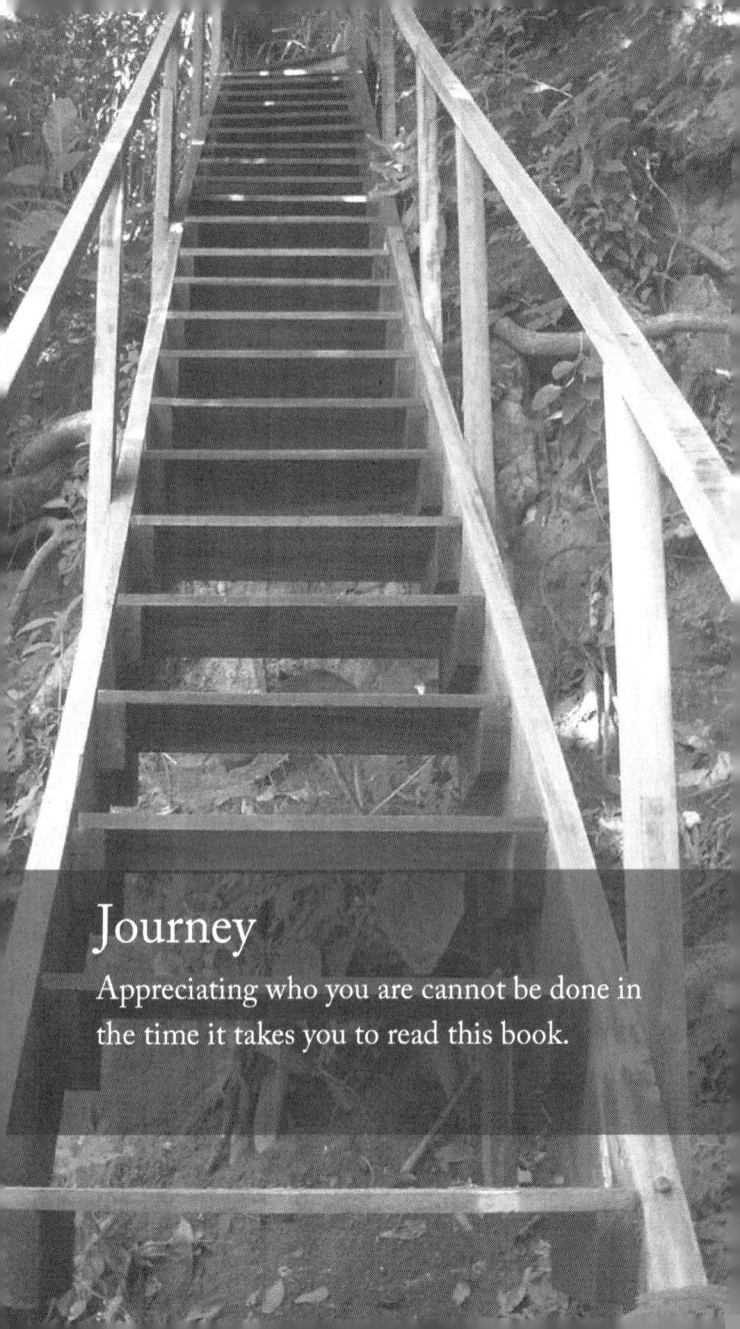

Appreciating who you are cannot be done in the time it takes you to read this book.

I have included within these covers some of the key things I have discovered in my life to date. This is the result of my age, having lived in three different countries and my experience of three career paths including the study of psychology, sociology and counselling. So it is an accumulation of my experience so far and undoubtedly part of my life's journey.

What has your life journey been like so far and have you begun to make sense of it? Is it all ahead of you or all behind you? How does that affect your day-to-day choices? For me I am grateful to my past and hopeful about my future whilst feeling that my current opportunities are good enough. It is up to me to make the best of what is available to me rather than focusing on what is imperfect. (Imperfection is part of the human condition and provides us all with opportunities to be vulnerable). I certainly feel that I am now on my individual life journey even though I don't know what happens next. Do you have a sense of having a past, present and future?

The sense of life being a journey can help us gain perspective. If we use the metaphor of travel then we can appreciate that sometimes we will like the scenery and other times we really want to get out of town. Some paths are easy to walk through and others require us to accept assistance. We may see others on our journey who appear to be having an easier or more difficult time. Making comparisons can be a distraction to keeping on our own path. We may feel we are running a marathon or a short sprint, doing hurdles or mountain climbing! Henry David Thoreau says that 'what lies behind us and what lies ahead of us are tiny matters compared to what lives within us.'

What opportunities do our journeys present for us and for those we meet? How do we cope with the difficulties and the privileges? What do we protect and what can we share with others we meet on the way? Maybe we can only appreciate a journey when we've got to the end and reflected on where we have been. It may be that we have time at the end to do this or it may be that others do that for us. It does not matter; our journey is ours and no one else's.

✏️ …

Kindness

For me kindness is a good quality to practice on our journey. The Bible talks about doing unto others as you would have them do unto you. But there is also something to be said for being kind whilst not expecting anything.

I am not talking here about the modern phenomenon of random acts of kindness where someone pays for a stranger's coffee (although that does have a place). For me kindness is simply about saying yes to a request that we can accommodate or offering to do something that we know will help another person. It could be as simple as picking up someone's shopping, watering their plants, giving them a lift, phoning to check that they are okay. It is about allowing someone else's situation to cross our mind and allowing ourselves to offer to ease their burden without feeling superior or heroic. It is sharing the gifts and resources that we have.

We may find ourselves on the receiving end of such generosity, and that is fine too. John Donne wrote that 'no man is an island' and it helps us to remember that our lives are all connected. Unfortunately it often takes a tragedy to remind us of this. I am not talking here of sacrificial giving and tithing which has its place for those of us with particular beliefs. Sometimes giving of our time and energy has more of an impact than writing a cheque. I am reminded here of a television program called The Secret Millionaire, where wealthy people go undercover to discover real needs and later, financially support these. I know they can get publicity from the show but as they already have a high profile in their field I do not think that is their motivation. It seems to me that they want to help and to feel the joy of giving. There are of course many who give of their time quietly through caring and volunteering.

Kindness is not about wealth. We are all capable of giving of ourselves, whoever we are, wherever we live. Is kindness something you experience of yourself or from those around you? Would you like to be kind to others or do you see that as being gullible? Are you very kind to some and unkind to others? How do you decide who or what to be kind to? Is there a person or project in your life that you could show kindness to?

✏️ ...

Laughter

So if you are feeling kind you can humour me with this joke. What is black and white and read all over? A newspaper!

Yes, I know that is not a very funny joke and that is why I am not a comedian. But humour is part of what makes life pleasurable. Smiling and laughing is good for our heart and helps us to de-stress. It does not get rid of the stresses altogether but offers some respite from them and is enjoyable in its own right. It can make us feel happy.

Psychologists and others have spent time analysing humour and why we find certain things funny. What you find funny can say a lot about who you are. If you spend enough time listening to comedians you can see the punch line as it approaches. That does not make it any less funny.

Do you laugh because of what you hear when someone tells a joke or is it about what you see. Many of the early silent movies are very entertaining to look at. With the growth of the internet humour now crosses a broad territory. I don't think humour is about picking on any one person or making fun of a group of people. That is unnecessary and cruel. Generally I prefer my humour in situation comedy or clever stand-ups with witty word play. But often it is the silliest things that remain in our memories.

Comedy does not have to be performed for us. Laughter can come from our everyday encounters with the people in our life. This can provide many private episodes of riotous laughter. We can always laugh at ourselves too. In surveys women often say that they want a man with a sense of humour although men don't seem to rate this as important for them. I do not know why that is.

I am glad I know what makes me laugh and I know where to find it. Is there a place for laughter in your life? Do you enjoy having a laugh or are you far too serious? Could you laugh with the ones you love?

✎ …

Love

The Bible says that God is love and sacrificed Jesus because he loved us so much. William Shakespeare refers to music as the food of love in Twelfth Night. Sigmund Freud identifies it in Eros as life's energy force. Others say love (and money) makes the world go around. Hollywood tells us that we all want to fall in love, as many times as necessary. Some of us are in love with love.

There are probably as many views of love as there are people on the planet. Great writing, music, art, film, dance and architecture have been inspired by love and serve as a monument to its expression. Love is powerful. Oprah Winfrey says that experiences presents us with an opportunity 'to choose love over fear.'

Love is certainly part of human need, desire and longing. Some of us are lucky enough to experience it at some point in our lives, and others are not. Maybe loving others starts with loving ourselves. In order to give and receive love we need to be able to trust ourselves and trust another. Can we love if we know that our feelings will not be reciprocated? Some people find it easy to love their children, family and friends; others do not. I have heard parents say that they would be prepared to die for their children: real sacrificial love.

Love may be both about who and what we attach ourselves to. We may have been badly hurt by our earlier attempts to love and be loved. Consequently we may find it easier to love power, status and material possessions. We can find ourselves becoming addicted to that which we once loved, or we might assume we love something because we are unhealthily addicted to it. Love is mysterious and can turn into hate.

Who or what do you love and how does that affect how you relate to them? Does it feel like a healthy love or more of the obsessive kind? Have you been damaged by love and need to heal before you can love again? Do you not love anyone because you are afraid of exposing yourself to the pain of disappointment? Are you missing out on beautiful emotional connections because you fear it will all go wrong?

Do your actions express what is in your heart? There is no need to love everything or everyone but to be open to the possibility seems important to me.

✎ ...

Money

Money is something many of us get very excited about. Generally people who do have money say it is not the most important thing in life and those who do not have money think it is.

Many of the things that make us happy cannot be bought, but a comfortable lifestyle can make it easier to maintain relationships. Only you can know what role money plays in your life and why it has this position. How much of this is about you and how much is due to how you were brought up? What was fine for you back then may not be appropriate anymore and you need to be able to see this and act on it accordingly. If money becomes your only goal in life then, not surprisingly, other things will suffer and deteriorate. How we relate to money affects our generosity, ability to receive, possessions, status and the choices we make.

Personally there have been times when I have earned a decent salary and wasted it chasing after ever changing fashionable clothes. At other times I have had little money but enjoyed free pursuits such as a walk in the park or by the river. I could be positive about this but I was never really at the risk of being homeless or starving and that must be a very stressful place to be.

In difficult times such as war, no amount of money can guarantee fair food distribution or home security. Then money just becomes bits of paper whilst influence becomes the more valued currency. So money is of no value in itself but only for what it can purchase. Food, shelter and relationships are valuable in their own right: life sustaining.

What is your relationship to the money in (or not in) your life? Is it the thing you spend all your time thinking about or does it come much lower down in your priorities? There is no right or wrong answer here. It depends on where you are starting from, your expectations and responsibilities.

✏️ ...

Mothers and Fathers

Like most things in life we learn about love and emotions in our early years. Many psychologists and analysts have documented the role of the mother in this.

Our mother's presence or not is critical to our early development. It can affect our relationships with other women whether we are male or female. But mothers are not solely responsible for child rearing, our fathers are important too. It is about recognising the impact these early years have had on who we are now and what we might need to do to continue to develop and grow. It seems silly to get into old age and still be blaming your parents for the bad start they gave you. At some point it is up to us to heal our own wounds so that we can move on. Parents often parent the way they were parented or they may become the exact opposite of their parents. What sort of parenting did you have and how has it affected you? If you are a parent, how has it influenced you?

Is there a quality, expectation, thought pattern or behaviour that you need to change because it is no longer helpful to your life even though it was essential in your family of origin? Are you still trying to get the approval of your parents or siblings or are you now travelling on your own path and being true to who you are? How does this early environment still affect what you believe you deserve and the subsequent choices you make?

If you feel there is something here to explore then you can arrange to see a therapist. This is confidential and you do not need to tell anyone. What would it be like if you could really become your best self? How would it be if people began to compliment you as they noticed a change? The real you could be hiding underneath lots of 'shoulds' and 'should nots'. You may discover that your whole life so far seems more like a dream than reality. Do you need to find a new home, job, relationship or purpose?

✎ …

Nature

Life is also about our connection to nature. What does the word nature conjure up for you? For some people it might be farm animals, dirt and smells. For others it is a country walk and a picnic.

We cannot spend whole days only gazing about noticing what is changing, but having some sense of what is happening in our environment is healthy and nature is part of that environment. Many studies show that we become a lot calmer when we have access to green spaces or the sound of flowing water. This is an easy and often free way to recharge our batteries. I am convinced that wherever we are we can find some connection to nature even if it is just going outside and looking up at the sky.

Like many of the other awakenings we have looked at you may decide that nature is quite important to you and this could affect your decision about where you live and the type of job that you do. As a careers adviser I have discussed the impact of job environment with my clients. If you enjoy nature you are more likely to become a farmer in a rural area than an office worker in a city. An office worker in a city could still include nature by incorporating a short walk, going jogging etc. Looking after a pet, such as taking a dog for a walk, could also encourage engagement with the natural world.

I enjoy picnics and I have several friends who love camping. I also like walking and for the past two years I have been getting into planting flowers. There is something very affirming about planting something and seeing it grow. Much of nature is free and available; we can enjoy it without owning it.

Are you someone who often pays attention to the changes in your natural environment such as weather, trees, plants, flowers, rivers, lakes, mountains and animals? On the other hand, do you only notice the new shopping centre, restaurant, supermarket or cinema? Do you feel a connection to your environment or do you drown it out with noise and lights? Can you be still and feed your soul or do you feel uneasy when the birds sing and the rivers flow?

✏️ ...

Openness

You may not have thought of nature before but you may have already been open to all that is happening around you. Some people are very open and take in much of what is happening in their immediate world and the world at large.

There is a lot going on and it is not possible to remain open to everything all the time so some choices need to be made. Nowadays we are expected to retain more and more information but such volume is probably not very healthy. We may feel the need to protect ourselves from things that make us feel vulnerable and powerless. That could be crime, the rise of racist political parties, the state of the global economy etc. Where we draw the line will have a significant impact for us. For example, I am open to fair trade and environmental concerns because I believe that my actions matter and contribute to the collective decisions made. Others may feel that the situation is futile and choose to close off and bury their heads in the sand. The belief affects the behaviour, which then has an impact on the environment.

Some of us believe we are very fragile so we live in an overly protected and closed space that may begin to lose its life energy. If we block off everything around us then our life will be quite limited and dull. We might also appear unreal and disconnected. Some level of openness and engagement is healthy.

Others of us want to know everything that is going on in the world, and we pack in so much that we give ourselves no space to discover what is going on within. We are open to so much that nothing really has a chance to connect to our inner world.

When we are truly open to new experiences then new things can come into our lives. For me I have found that quite refreshing. It may be as simple as befriending someone who is not like anyone you are normally friends with. Sometimes it is about leaving gaps in our plans so that we can take up the suggestion of another. Openness implies some flexibility and spontaneity in how we live our lives.

There are new technologies, new knowledge and new experiences which we might need to be aware of even if we do not experience them all. Openness will allow for new people and ideas to be included in your world. For instance, there have been new insights into how the brain works and how to keep healthy which all of us could benefit from understanding. If we are not open to personal growth (and associated change) then we fix ourselves to a very staid and dull existence.

Like everything mentioned here it is still about balance. Being open does not mean attaching yourself to every change that comes along. To me it means having some constant centre whilst being able to appraise new ideas and experiences as they come along, accepting some and rejecting others. That's true freedom. The two extremes of accept everything or accept nothing can become automatic and unhelpful.

✎ …

Passion

We also benefit from discovering our passion. Many of the other things we have looked at so far could also impact on your passion such as your attitude, your beliefs, your sense of identity and your early environment.

Finding your passion can be achieved through careers guidance, counselling and some spiritual or other types of retreat. It is not so important how you get there but that you do take time to discover what your passion might be. Tony Robbins sees passion as 'the genesis of genius'.

That does not mean you must spend the rest of your life focusing on your passion to the exclusion of everything else. Volunteering is a wonderful way to explore your various ideas. It may be that it starts off as a hobby before it grows into something you will be paid for. Whatever the case other tasks of life still need to be done. For most of us routine monotonous tasks have to be done even if we have found our passion. If you are wealthy enough you can hire people to cut your grass and do your laundry but sometimes those simple tasks help to slow us down and calm our minds giving us some reflective space.

If you are passionate about something you will happily do it for free. People often say that about the arts in particular. There are lots of people who create and perform just for the fun of it. I regularly go to the Edinburgh Fringe festival and I see so many students thoroughly enjoying presenting their production even though they do not make a lot of money from it. Of course we are so caught up with celebrity now that it is difficult to separate the passionate from the wannabe.

There are also teachers, health workers, lawmakers and advisers from many backgrounds who have a passion for their work and continue in the face of incredible hurdles. It presents a wonderful reason for getting out of bed every day. Are you passionate about anything at the moment? Have you ever been passionate about anything? Would you like to be passionate about something in the future?

✏️ ...

Personality

For some of us our passions may not feel like a simple choice but more the result of personality and the people we have met along the way.

Personality is a very complex thing and there are several psychological tests that try to assess people's personality type. The one I value is Myers-Briggs, which came out of the work of Carl Jung.

It's too much to go into here but it suggests that some people are introverts (they get energy from being on their own) and some are extroverts (they get energy from being with other people). Just in this simple way we can see how differences would affect our relationships. If two such individuals are brought up in the same family then it doesn't take much for them to experience the same family experiences in a very different way.

Personality affects how we see ourselves and how others see us. All types can like or dislike people. I could be in a crowd thinking I am better than everyone and I could be on my own thinking how wonderful people are, or vice versa. It is useful to have some sense of our personality at any given time as this can change as a result of life's experiences. This may help us avoid situations when we are shocked by our own behaviour.

When we understand how we function we can find ways to maximise our input into life and to build our self-esteem. If we discover that we hate noisy public events then we can seek out small quiet events and feel more comfortable. They could both be for the same cause but just done differently. For example, you could protest for Amnesty International in person or you could quietly help them stuff envelopes for fundraising: both of these help the organisation but your input would be different depending on your personality. If you find yourself with the wrong group of people for your disposition then it could feel very uncomfortable and isolating. It is good to know that there are other personalities that would really suit you.

Society is organised in such a way that those who get their energy from being with people do not ever have to be alone; they can go from one group to the next without a break. This means that they continue to develop the part of their personality that they are already comfortable with and never have to work on the other. On the other hand, those who get their energy from being alone cannot remain on their own all the time. They must also develop their ability to be with groups of people if they wish to function with family, work and relationships.

I know an American woman who thought she was an extrovert until she moved to England and realised that the American culture made her behave in an extroverted way but that was not really her true self. Sometimes couples see each other differently after they are married. Is it that a partner's personality has changed or that the viewer is seeing differently? Have you got a sense of your personality? Is this how you have always been or a recently discovered way of seeing yourself? Are there parts of you that you still don't know or understand?

✏️ ...

Play

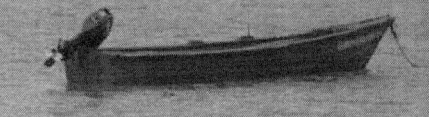

Our personality influences how we play. Such fun activities are a good way to enhance our experience of living.

It has a vital role from childhood through to adulthood. It is telling that I forgot to include this in my first draft. I have been more serious than I have needed to be throughout my life and have recently begun to catch up on my play. In some ways play was always there in my life but I saw it as free time. Nevertheless it was an opportunity to be creative and not perform to schedule. Play can encourage learning and learning can be done as play.

Play is creative and expressive. It gives us an opportunity to step outside ourselves and relax. It is about fun and laughter, all part of a fulfilling life. A sense of humour is key to having fun at play. Although play at school is different from play at work play continues throughout life. Childhood will affect our relationship to this but left alone children will play. Sports, music, drama, dance and board games can be an easy way into structured play. Spontaneous play or fooling around is a more advanced skill, which takes years of time wasting to perfect! It could simply be about being and not doing. For me this could be as frivolous as dressing up and painting my nails! It is simply about being human and letting go of self-importance. Those who play together can also build better relationship bonds and create memories. Have a go – it's fun!

Whilst my play has been too little there are others who are all play and no work. For all of us balance is important. What has been your experience of play, too much or too little? How could you bring a better balance if necessary? Do you know someone at the opposite end of your spectrum that you can pair up with to bring more balance to both of you?

✏ …

Quiet spaces

It is important to have time to reflect on what our life is, the journey we are on and where we are heading. It is about stopping and enjoying the moment.

I recently heard a lot of praise about going slow, which is an antidote to all the rushing around and multitasking that many of us do.

I do not believe that human beings are designed to go as fast as we are trying to. We are presented with hundreds of choices every day from emails, posters, supermarkets, outfits and travel options to name but a few. I am like every one else – trying to absorb everything so that I can make the best choice. Sometimes it is simply not worth the effort and takes up valuable down time.

Another way of slowing down is to engage in the practice of meditation. Many great thinkers and spiritual people find this a rewarding experience. Although we think of meditation in the context of Buddhism I believe Christians and other faiths also have a place for meditation in their belief systems. It is also possible to meditate and not belong to any faith group.

There are lots of resources and centres that can tell you more about the practice and benefits of meditation. 'Your sacred space is where you can find yourself again and again.' Joseph Campbell. I do know that it helps us to slow down and find peace within ourselves and we can then carry this into the world through our daily encounters. I do not meditate as regularly as I would like but whenever I do I am never disappointed.

So we need to give ourselves time for being rather than only doing. Part of the problem we get caught up in is the need to tell others what we did on the weekend or bank holiday, for our birthday or an anniversary. What will our friends say if we told them we spent the weekend listening to music, writing poetry or meditating? Are we always busy so we don't appear boring? If we don't give ourselves time to reflect how do we know why we are doing what we are doing? I think that quiet times help us on our quest to a fulfilling life that connects to our values.

Throughout this I am also encouraging us to ask questions of ourselves, and those in our life. It is not good to accept what others tell us we should be doing. Socrates says that 'the unexamined life is not worth living'. This whole book is dedicated to asking questions of ourselves and then honestly seeking out the answers. This seeking is what makes our life uniquely ours and offers vitality, authenticity and genuine freedom.

✎ ...

Relationships

It is not all about seeking; we can relax and consider our relationships. Who is important to us and how would they know this?

I know it can feel embarrassing telling people that we care about them but we need to find our own way of conveying this to them. Imagine if they died and did not know how you felt about them. Similarly do you know the people in your life who really care about you? Regardless of how successful or rich we might become, life is enjoyed when we have people to celebrate our successes and empathise with our challenges. I feel that good relationships are key to an enjoyable life.

As I get older this is something I have improved upon. I love to have intimate birthday parties where I invite close friends who are important to me. As time has gone on and life has presented its tragedies it is important to know that there are people who I can lean on and who could lean on me. This is not really about mutual support because different people offer different things to a relationship but it is about a sense of awareness, where we do the best we can to be good spouses, friends, family, colleagues, neighbours etc. We can take responsibility for our part in our relationships. For Carl Jung 'the meeting of two personalities is like the contact of two chemical substances: if there is any reaction, both are transformed.'

Your way will probably be different from my way but it is important for you that you know how to do it for your circle of relations. Best to be a little awkward and let people know how you feel about them rather than risk them thinking you do not care. This is not about buying friendships or performing affection to onlookers but about having an honest encounter with people in your life.

Having good relationships does not mean that everyone is always smiles and happiness. It is about being true with each other. So many people go through life without getting honest feedback because no one in their life cares enough (or is brave enough) to tell them when they are behaving inappropriately. If the first time you are given such feedback is at school or work then it has a public element to it that may make it more difficult to accept. Challenging feedback is probably best delivered in love and privately.

It is important to have people in our lives who can encourage us to grow, learn, deepen and be our best self. What are you doing to attract such people into your life and to be that friend to the people in your life? For that you need honesty, trust, care and courage, but the resulting impact can be phenomenal. I have experienced this through my counselling training and my small church group as well as with longstanding individual friendships and peer groups. As I get older they all become more important and valued. The truth is that no money in the world could buy quality relationships.

How do you communicate to let people know that you appreciate, value and respect them? Do you spend time nourishing your relationships or do you expect them to stay alive by themselves?

✎ ...

Responsibility

We need to take responsibility for the state of our relationships and our lives as a whole.

When we are children, we are under the control of our parents, siblings and school and we have limited power to affect our environment. Once we begin to have some control over our life then we need to become aware of the quality and quantity of our relationships and have a sense of how our behaviour can have an impact on these. Do you want to know lots of people in a shallow way or to know a few people really well? Like me you may want both but in reality this is hard to achieve.

If your early experiences make it difficult to make friends or trust people then it is possible to discuss this with someone who can help. Maybe you need to move to a new place and start over. Maybe you need to figure out what you are interested in and find other people who are also keen on your hobby. Gaining confidence with like-minded people will help you with people in general and relationships will probably get easier over time. Intimate relationships may also need attention and again the approach is the same; explore your expectations (therapy or counselling), increase your awareness of and openness to such relationships and it will become easier. Empower yourself to find out how you work in this way and take steps to be all that you can be. You do not have to repeat the mistakes you may have witnessed around you.

No one is perfect and you do not need to be but it would be good if you could allow yourself to continue to learn and grow. It always amazes me that we learn so much from age ten to age twenty and yet expect to learn very little in subsequent decades. This is not only about world knowledge but self-knowledge too. We run around looking for answers and we carry them within ourselves. Do you feel you take responsibility for your life? Are you blaming others for the life you now lead? How can you take responsibility to make the right choices for yourself? Are you inhibited because you fear making a choice that you later regret?

✎ ...

Safety

In order for us to begin to look internally we really need to feel safe. From a place of safety we can look within at who we are and reach out to others in the knowledge that we can meet with them authentically.

Safety and food are amongst our basic needs. Abraham Maslow refers to this in his hierarchy of needs. He suggests that once we meet these basic needs, then we can work our way through our belonging and esteem needs. He sees the pinnacle as self-actualisation when we are achieving our full potential.

So safety is crucial to our personal development. If you feel unsafe in your current situation I hope you can make changes so that your circumstances become safer. Hopefully there is someone you can speak to who can support you in your quest.

The bigger picture is about helping to make the world safer for all of us. Certainly life has always had its fair share of danger but the quality and quantity of it seems to be changing all the time. I am unlikely to be attacked by a wild animal or die of malaria but, unfortunately, I can easily be caught up in a traffic accident. The people we know and listen to affect how safe we feel but we can't really hide ourselves away from reality. For me it is about making the best judgement I can, when considering activities, associated risks and pleasure. There is no point trying to be completely safe but not living.

The trend at the moment seems to be about taking bodily risks with adrenaline fuelled activities. The body responds to the unnaturalness of the activity (e.g. bungee jumping) but the organised nature of the event means that it is likely to be safe. This can be seen more like the organised play I mentioned earlier. I confess to be scared of participating in many of these activities and this is a work in progress for me.

How do you feel about your own safety? Is it something you worry about or does it not impact on your thoughts at all? If you live in fear how is that affecting your life? Is there anything or anyone that could help you to feel safer so that you can participate in life more fully?

So my alphabet soup of life is almost complete. You may be getting distracted from the content and wondering how I will cope with the latter letters. Well you will have to wait and see. Before I progress however there is another 'S' that I want to mention: Soul. I know one stereotype of Black people is that we have soul; I believe we all have soul. The truth is that some of us do not want to take time to connect to ourselves on such a deep level.

🖉 …

Soul

Soul is part of our heart's connection to the depths of our being and how we are enabled to live this truth.

For me it is about colour, scenery, food, art, language, music and dance. They feed my soul with their rich expressions and tones. I am not great at any (except eating) but I love to engage with them. Significant relationships and my faith also really connect to my inner being. For others it may be about architecture, design and landscaping. For some it is being a mother or father.

Does anything get to the depths of your soul? What really makes you feel alive?

🖉 …

Thinking

Rene Descartes said 'I think therefore I am.' As you can see from what we have looked at so far, to be really engaged in your life you need to engage your mind in thinking about what you do, who you do it with and how what you are doing lives up to your beliefs.

I don't like the idea of sleepwalking through life, especially already having done a bit of that in my teens.

Thinking is important. It encourages learning and using our individual skills to resolve our own problems rather than trying to be like everyone else.

There have been great thinkers in our world over many centuries. There are great philosophers, politicians, scientists and mathematicians. There are those who explain how the human mind works, how groups behave and how to design clever things such as spacecrafts, robots and submarines.

We need to trust ourselves to believe we can solve our issues. So many people have been told they are no good that they no longer trust themselves, which means that they are always looking outside themselves for their answers. In my work as a counsellor I try to help people in growing their self-esteem and confidence so that they can trust themselves. It takes time, mostly undoing all the negative comments they have received in their life to date, but it is possible.

How do use your mind? Are you able to think things through when making decisions? Could you be making more of your thinking capacity? Is there something you would like to learn more about?

✏️ ...

Time

Time is something we can do nothing about. We cannot quicken it or slow it down. We do not know how long we have but we have the gift of each day and it is up to us to make choices about how we use that time.

Work, relationships and activities may take up a lot of our time but hopefully these things bring us security, joy, fun and a sense of belonging amongst others. Some of us are so busy we feel there aren't enough hours in each day. Others are unemployed and alone and struggle to fill empty days. We all have the same 24 hours in each day.

How do you spend your 24 hours? Does it feel like you have any choices or none at all? If it feels like you have no choice at all then you might need to have a look at how you prioritise the things you spend time on. Whose life are you living and what sort of expectations gain precedence? If you found you had a spare hour what would you use it for? Relaxation, housework, sleeping, fitness, reading, listening to audio, D-I-Y, watching a film or meeting up with a friend?

Generally, do you do the same things all the time? How would it be to try something different for more variety? I am excited and scared by the things I can't yet do and hope, plan and intend to do in the future. I still want to learn to play an instrument and learn a language. It is not beyond me but I need to make space for it. That may mean I have less time to listen to the radio or watch television or films. What would you like to do with your time that you are not doing at the moment, and how might you be able to do this?

✎ ...

Understanding

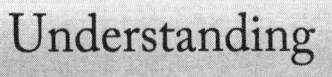

If we are going to be building relationships, learning, growing and changing our environments, life will become less straightforward for many of us.

When we meet someone new we cannot know where they are in their personal journey, what they might need from us, or we from them.

It strikes me that we need a great deal of understanding of ourselves, and each other. Some of us are good at showing understanding to others and tend to value individuality and difference. Other people like everyone to be the same, preferably similar to them. But we are all on different paths in our journey of life so why do we judge others by our own journey? Understanding enables us to be more honest to the variety of choices and possibilities there are without feeling that our way is worst or best, just different.

Sometimes we give a lot of attention to visible differences such as race, gender, religion and disability, but hidden differences can have as big an impact on our daily experiences. Think of someone who hears voices or has certain food allergies and how they would experience their world differently to how they would be viewed from the outside. With understanding we can find empathy for others and empathy for ourselves. Studies show that when we are harsh on others we tend to be harsh on ourselves too.

Do you try to be understanding of the people you meet in your daily life? Would you like to do this more often or less often?

✏️ …

Values

Such understanding implies versatility in approach. This does not mean being so versatile that you stand for nothing. Here we need to look at our values. Your values are the things in life that you hold dear; behavioural standards you hold for yourself and for others.

If honesty is a value then you don't need to tolerate liars in your relationships. Your most authentic approach would be to tell them that you cannot be in a relationship with them because you have found out that they do not speak truthfully and you are unable to trust them. Without trust the relationship becomes superficial and your time is too precious for that. Maya Angelou observes that 'courage is the most important of all the virtues, because without courage you can't practice any other virtue consistently. You can practice any virtue erratically, but nothing consistently without courage'.

Values are linked to right and wrong and moral codes of behaviour. Sometimes we can figure out what we think and feel in conversation with others. This relies on having quality relationships built on openness and trust, as discussed earlier. As you may be beginning to realise, these all link together in some way. Where can you start?

Start with exploring yourself and maybe your unmet needs, those which you would love to have in your life but have not been able to attract. It could be safety, trust, love, home etc. This could then lead you to explore the values you hold dear. My values are key to how I try to live my life. It is about helping people to live the best and fullest life they can whether that is through careers advice, therapy, teaching or writing. It is about healing our relationships and healing ourselves. I am saddened by waste whether that is a wasted life, skills, resources or opportunities. My values link to my belief that we are all created with unique gifts that we can offer to the world. This book is my attempt to contribute.

What are your values? Do these help you to make choices in your day-to-day life? How do you respond when these are challenged? Are your values realistic for normal people or are they only achievable by super humans? I have come across so many clients who set unrealistic standards for themselves. Are they your own values or ones that you have co-opted from other people? It is important to find your own true values to steer your life.

✏️ ...

Will

When we think of will we tend to think of will power and the idea of forcing ourselves to do something only because this would give others a favourable idea of us.

There are wonderful things in life that we may not want to do but need to do in order to live a fulfilled life. When faced with such tasks we need to find a way of engaging our will so that we can complete the task at hand. This may be for repetitive tasks at home such as cleaning or more important things such as setting goals or making a commitment. It could also be about making a significant life change such as giving up smoking or drugs. The initial decision is important but engaging the will helps us to stay on course with our decision.

Is there something that you would really like to add to your life but you are hesitant about committing to? Is there any thing or person or influence you would like to remove from your life but you don't believe you have what it takes to achieve this? Try using your will to help you through – it might work.

✎ ...

Witness

Sometimes it is not simply who we are and how we are but what other people make of us. Here I want to talk about being a witness to others, and being seen by others. The term is used in religious and legal circles but I am using it in a therapeutic way.

It's about seeing another as we witness their life. It is also about being seen by others as they witness our life. What is it like to be seen in our happiness or sadness, joy or frustration? Similarly, what is it like to really see others close to us go through the range of experiences and emotions that make up their life?

Before I became a counsellor I cannot say I was particularly conscious of this. I now know how powerful it is to witness others in their pain, for example, and to be seen with my feelings. We like to know that we are not alone and that people see that we are alive.

It's healthy to be heard and seen when we are struggling, and perhaps celebrated with when things are going well. Our peers may be in different places and that's where understanding, love and kindness come in. But the challenge is to witness to others when life is difficult for them. This is delicate and important. If you are having a difficult time it is made even worse if others see your difficulty and ignore it. This ignoring of their pain is like another blow to them saying that their pain does not matter.

Maybe we could recognise the daily struggles of those close to us, and how bravely they deal with their challenges. A compliment from us would let them know that we see their courage and vulnerability and admire them for it. By witnessing to them we are saying "yes it is real, you are not dreaming".

Having read this, is there anyone in your life you would like to say something to?

✎ …

(e)Xpress

So with all this openness, values and relationship building there is a lot to take in and a lot to eXpress. In all these ways we are trying to discover and express ourselves so that our life is true and authentic.

This is what makes us fulfilled and maybe even happy. It is extraordinarily simple and yet challenging at the same time.

Expressing yourself does not mean being a nuisance to others although you may offend on occasion (some people are very limited in their imaginations). I often find myself entertained by people who explore psychedelic colours, and dye their hair in, say, purple. I do not want to do it myself but I value their presence in my environment. They are proud to be different. How boring it would be if everyone wore jeans and a t-shirt or a suit!

It can take a while to discover who we are in different aspects of our lives. For Albert Einstein 'a person who never made a mistake never tried anything new'. I know people who can express themselves through cooking a meal or designing cards but not in dressing themselves. I myself enjoy exploring colour in my wardrobe but can become quite hesitant when it comes to using colour in my home. (I did paint a room red before changing it to sea blue when it became my therapy room!)

When we step into a new phase of our life it can take a while to express our new freedoms. It may be that previously a parent, landlord, housemate or spouse had dampened our expression.

You may find you explore in your twenties and thirties and revert back to earlier expressions in your middle years. I know apparently conservative people who used to be punks in their youth. Expression may become subtle over time. The loudness of youth may be replaced by soulful reflections of middle age or it could be the opposite. Only you know what is within that you would love to give life to. I am doing it here and now myself through the written word, even though I have no idea what will become of this. Expression can force itself through, having an impact on the lives of others and bringing about the unexpected.

So how about you, are you able to express yourself in any sphere of your life? Are there areas where you would like to express more of yourself? Is there anything you can do about this?

✎ …

Yearning

And so we come to yearning. We may be yearning for something different from what we have although we do not know what it is.

We may need to stop ourselves on the daily automatic existence that we have, to be conscious of our soul's yearning. What is it that we long for? It takes guts to stop and listen to our inner being; it is far easier to carry on working and shopping.

A yearning is not likely to be for a material thing, although that could be desired too. But you may yearn for space to be yourself, to be a parent, to travel the world, to create something from your own resources, to make a positive contribution to the world, to be able to trust someone. Ralph Waldo Emerson suggests that we 'do not go where the path leads, go instead where there is no path and leave a trail.'

Take time to reflect on what you yearn for. Does anything come to mind? Whatever you just thought of might be the thing you really want. How would it be to begin to explore the possibility of bringing that into your life?

✎ ...

Zero tolerance

So we have been encouraged to look at our lives in full and pay attention to who we are, how we behave and what we think. Add to this our beliefs, values, how we feel about others and ourselves. This is all positive and enhancing. But life is complex and full of shade and light.

Now I am going to look at zero tolerance. I am not thinking here of policing. I will not tell you what you should have zero tolerance towards, but if your values and beliefs are worth anything then there will be things in the world that will challenge what you stand for. Zero tolerance does not mean hurting someone who disagrees with you or causing violence but being able to say to yourself that there are certain things you disagree with.

Dr. Martin Luther King Jr said that 'Injustice anywhere is a threat to justice everywhere.' I myself find the concept of child soldiers intolerable. War is horrendous but even more so when it involves brutalising children and getting them to kill other children, setting up horror for the future. Their nightmares will continue to affect them and any family they might have. In fact I find all childhood abuse unacceptable as it corrupts innocence and takes human suffering forward to another generation. It does not make any sense. But to my shame I have not been involved in stopping this practice. If this is a value I have then I need to begin to do something. Their potential is being squashed and they are powerless to stop it. I could start small and see where it goes but I can no longer pretend that I do not know. Barack Obama says that 'change will not come if we wait for some other person or some other time. We are the ones we've been waiting for. We are the change that we seek'.

How about you? What is it that you no longer wish to tolerate? Homelessness? Poverty? People trafficking?

See what comes up for you and then think about how you can make a difference. This is not something to do before you try to figure out who you are. Sometimes it is easier to try to fix the world instead of looking at ourselves in the mirror. I really think it is healthier to sort out who we are first and know the limits and the reasons for our helping so that we do not lose ourselves in a cause and let our relationships go to ruin. We are of value in just being ourselves and we do not need to be heroic to be loved or accepted.

✏️ …

Ending

So here it is, my alphabet soup for life. It is all an interpretation of truths that I have picked up through my life and training. It has been a spontaneous exercise that I have enjoyed tremendously. It is a gift to you to do what you wish with. Take the parts that make sense to you and use them. Leave the rest. Now I am near the end I can feel my anxiety about giving this over and being open to the feedback that might come my way. I refused to think about that while I was writing because I did not know if I would finish and I recognised that such thoughts would make me guarded in my writing. Now that I am finished I can feel those thoughts creeping into my mind. Maybe that is the lesson here – live from your passion and deal with the feedback afterwards. You might then have fun and make an impact

– hopefully positive. I would like to end with another quote.

'Love must be sincere. Hate what is evil; cling to what is good. Be devoted to one another in brotherly love. Honour one another above yourselves. Never be lacking in zeal, but keep your spiritual fervour, serving the Lord. Be joyful in hope, patient in affliction, faithful in prayer. Share with God's people who are in need. Practise hospitality. Bless those who persecute you; bless and do not curse. Rejoice with those who rejoice; mourn with those who mourn. Live in harmony with one another. Do not be proud, but be willing to associate with people of low position. Do not be conceited. Do not repay anyone evil for evil. Be careful to do what is right in the eyes of everybody. If it is possible, as far as it depends on you, live at peace with everyone. Do not take revenge, my friends, but leave room for God's wrath, for it is written: "It is mine to avenge; I will repay," says the Lord. On the contrary: "If your enemy is hungry, feed him; if he is thirsty, give him something to drink. In doing this, you will heap burning coals on his head." Do not be overcome by evil, but overcome evil with good.'

ROMANS CHAPTER 12, VERSES 9–21 IN THE BIBLE (NEW INTERNATIONAL VERSION)

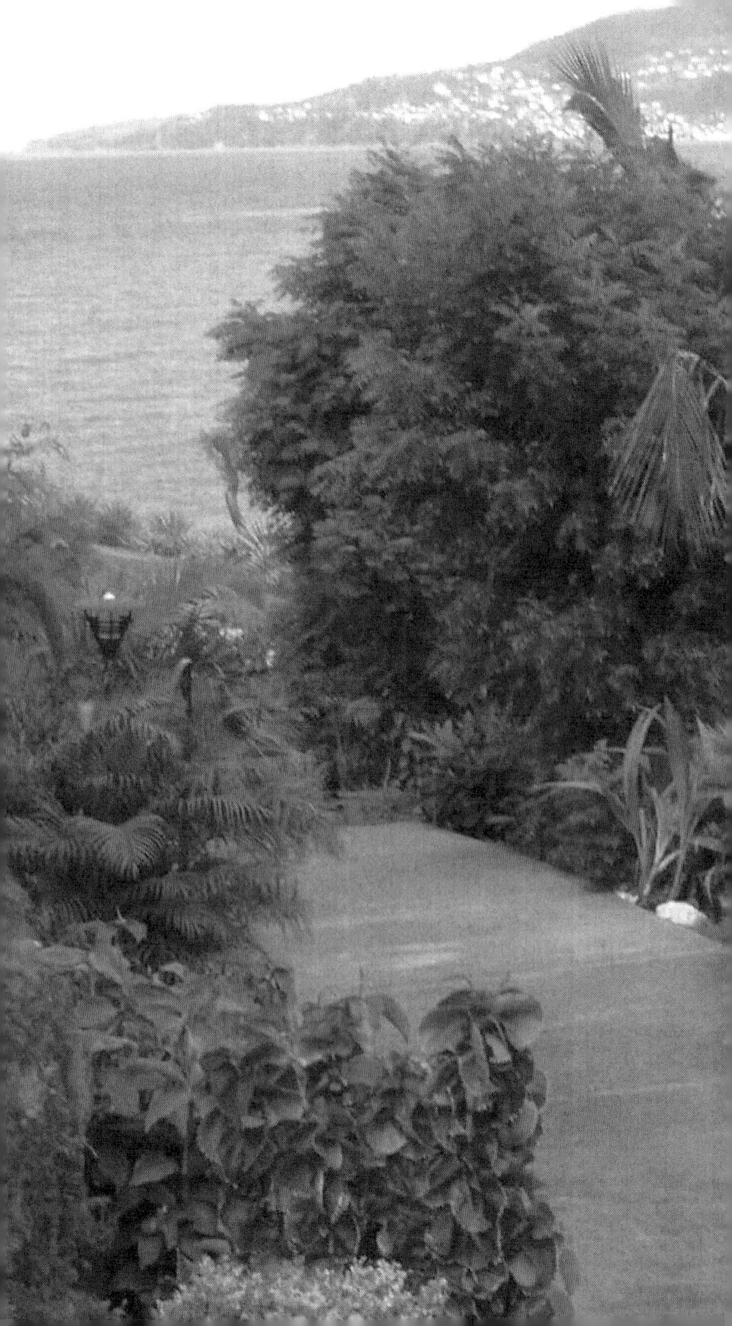

Our Greatest Fear

It is our light not our darkness that most frightens us.
Our deepest fear is not that we are inadequate.
Our deepest fear is that we are powerful beyond measure.
It is our light not our darkness that most frightens us.
We ask ourselves, who am I to be brilliant, gorgeous, talented and fabulous? Actually, who are you not to be?
You are a child of God.
Your playing small does not serve the world. There's nothing enlightened about shrinking so that other people won't feel insecure around you. We were born to make manifest the glory of God that is within us. It's not just in some of us; it's in everyone.
And as we let our own light shine, we unconsciously give other people permission to do the same. As we are liberated from our own fear, our presence automatically liberates others.

QUOTE FROM 'RETURN TO LOVE' BY MARIANNE
WILLIAMSON, HARPER COLLINS, 1992.
USED IN A SPEECH BY NELSON MANDELA.